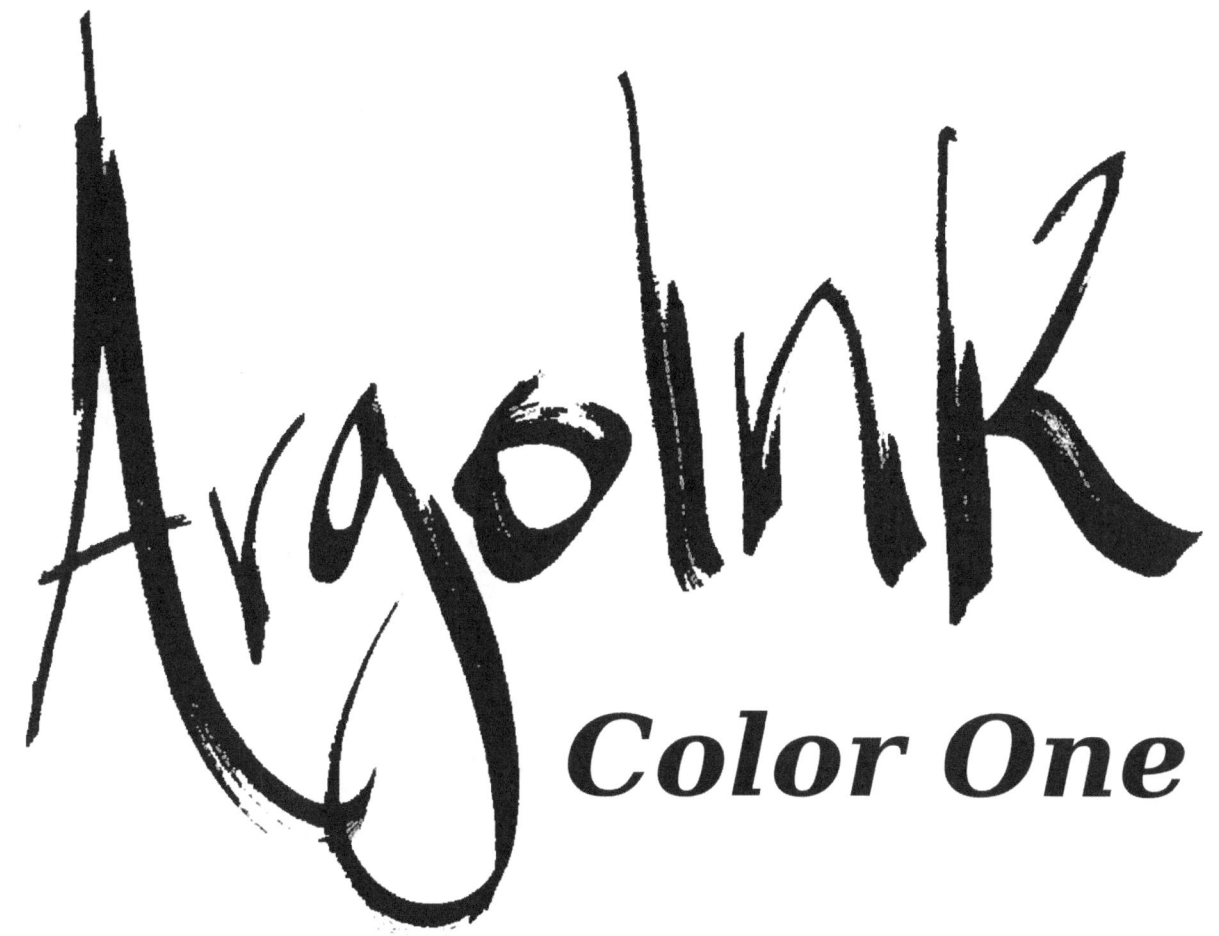

ArgoInk
Color One

Illustrated by

Chris Argo

ISBN-13: 978-1468150681
ISBN-10: 1468150685

http://www.ArgoInk.com

Dedicated to:

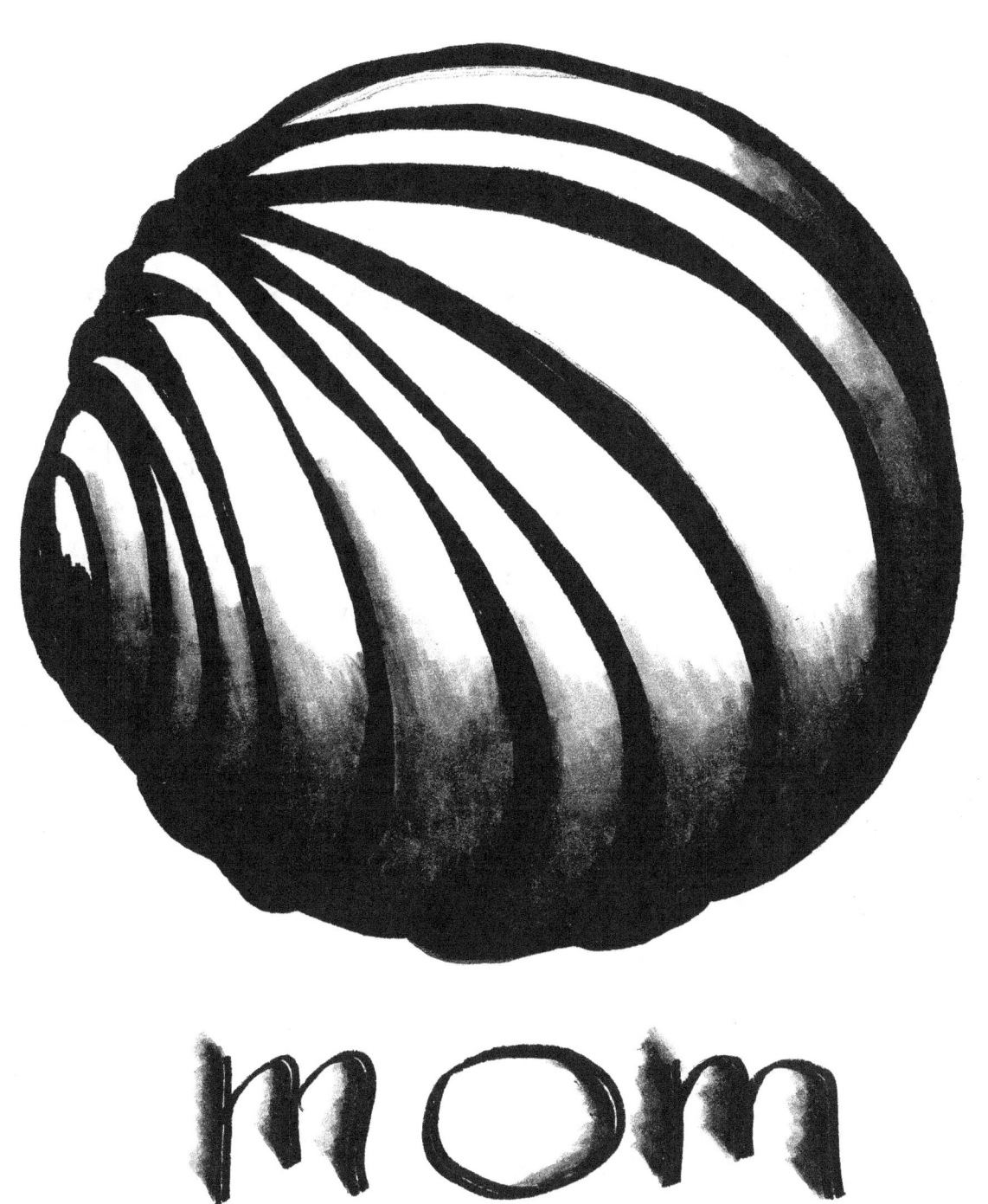

mom

"Our deepest fear is not that we are inadequate. Our deepest fear is that we are powerful beyond measure. It is our light, not our darkness that most frightens us. We ask ourselves, who am I to be brilliant, gorgeous, talented, fabulous? Actually, who are you NOT to be? You are a child of God. Your playing small does not serve the world. There is nothing enlightened about shrinking so that other people won't feel insecure around you. We are all meant to shine, as children do. We were born to make manifest the glory of God that is within us. It's not just in some of us; it's in everyone. And as we let our own light shine, we unconsciously give other people permission to do the same. As we are liberated from our own fear, our presence automatically liberates others."

-- Nelson Mandela

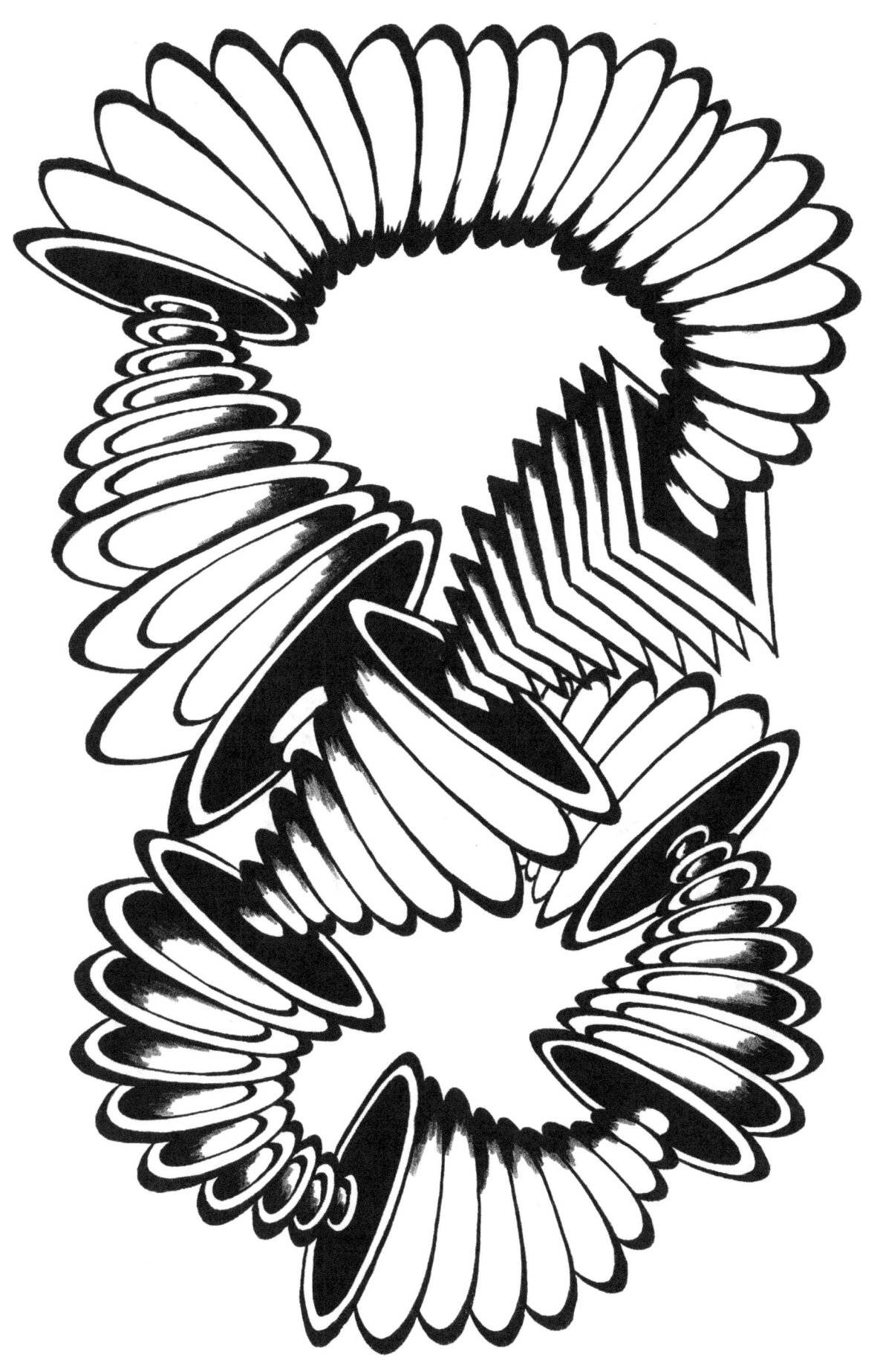

You will never do anything in this world without courage. It is the greatest quality of the mind next to honor.

Pleasure in the job puts perfection in the work.

Misfortune shows those who are not really friends.

Liars when they speak the truth are not believed.

Poverty is the parent of revolution and crime.

*-- **Aristotle (384 BC - 322 BC)***

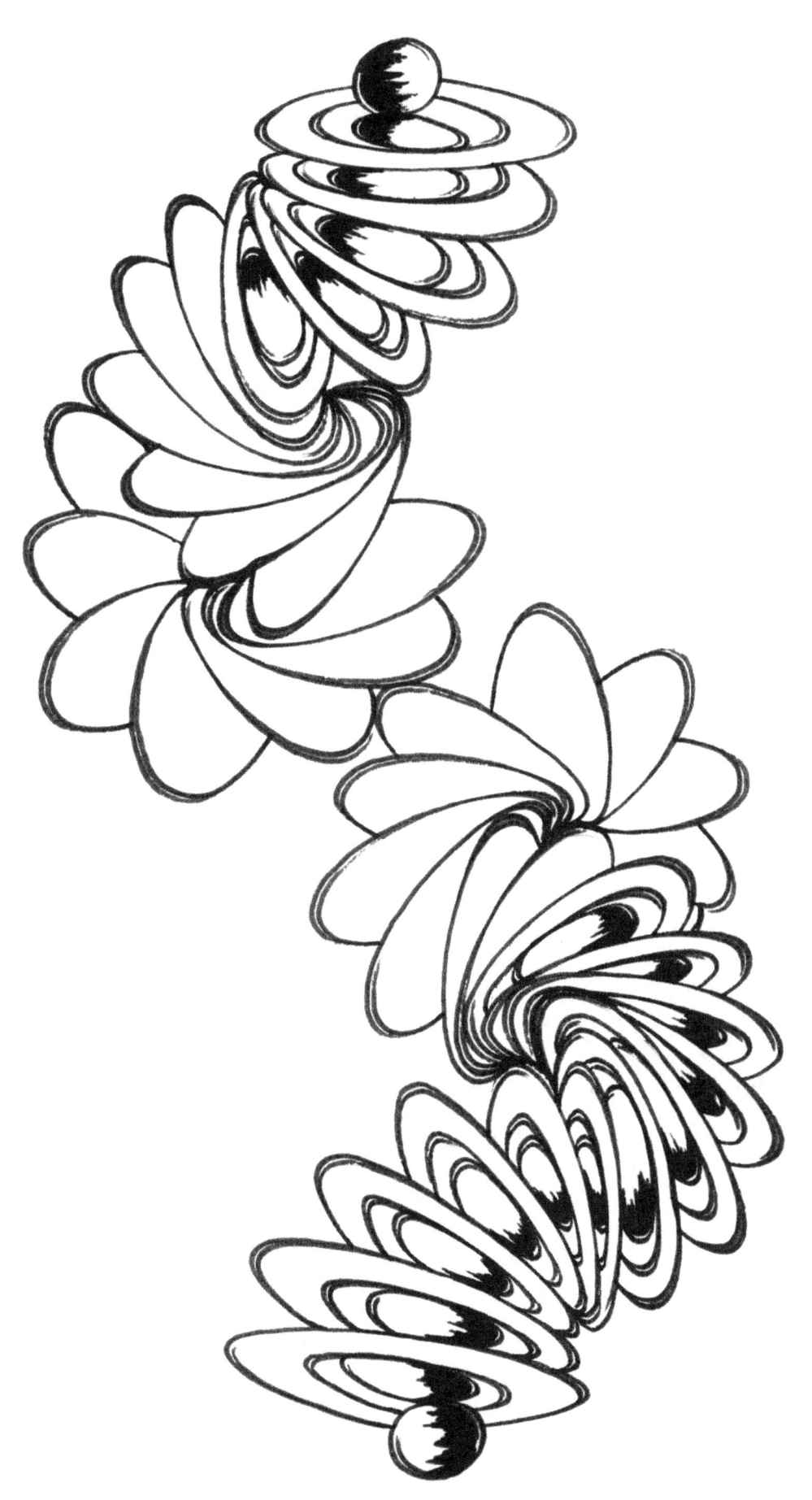

Nothing is easier than self-deceit. For what each man wishes, that he also believes to be true.

He who confers a favor should at once forget it, if he is not to show a sordid ungenerous spirit.

To remind a man of a kindness conferred and to talk of it, is little different from reproach.

Beware lest in your anxiety to avoid war you obtain a master.

Small opportunities are often the beginning of great enterprises.

The readiest and surest way to get rid of censure, is to correct ourselves.

What we have in us of the image of God is the love of truth and justice.

-- Demosthenes (384 BC - 322 BC)

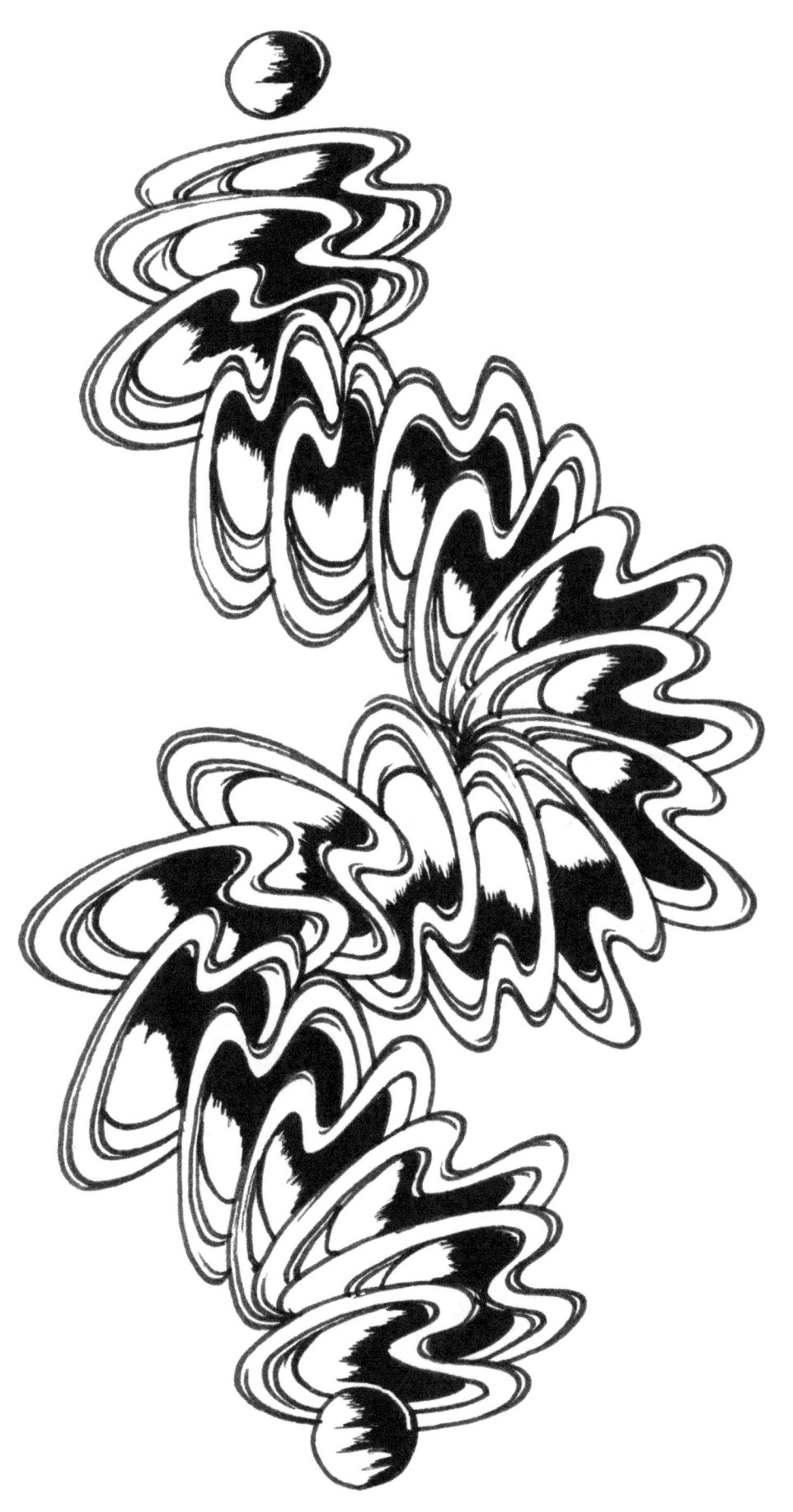

Wise men are instructed by reason; men of less understanding, by experience; the most ignorant, by necessity; the beasts, by nature.

A happy life consists in tranquility of mind.

Advice is judged by results, not by intentions.

Never go to excess, but let moderation be your guide.

-- Cicero (106 BC - 43 BC)

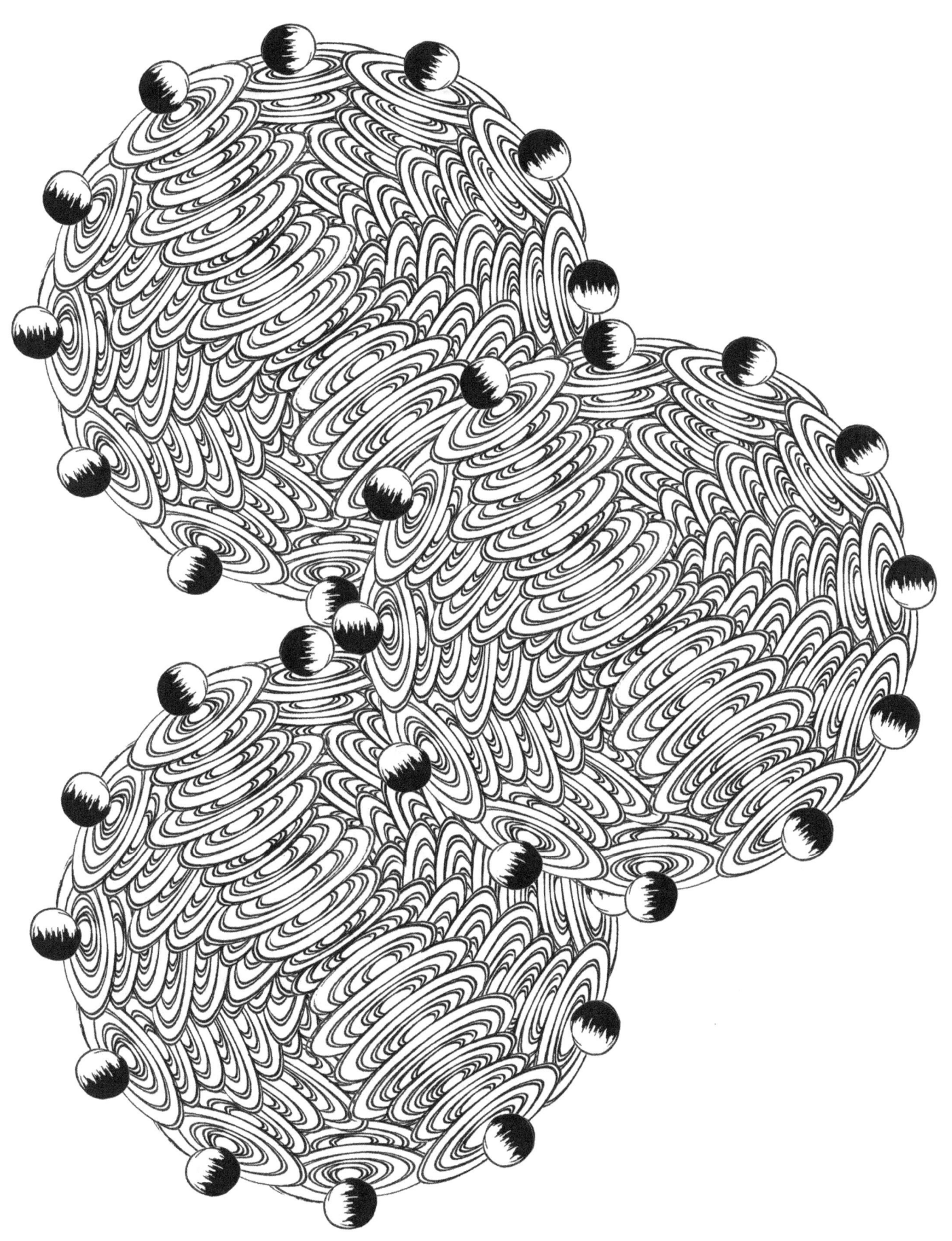

By three methods we may learn wisdom: First, by reflection, which is noblest; Second, by imitation, which is easiest; and third by experience, which is the bitterest.

Everything has its beauty but not everyone sees it.

He who will not economize will have to agonize.

Wheresoever you go, go with all your heart.

They must often change who would be constant in happiness or wisdom.

-- Confucius (551 BC - 479 BC)

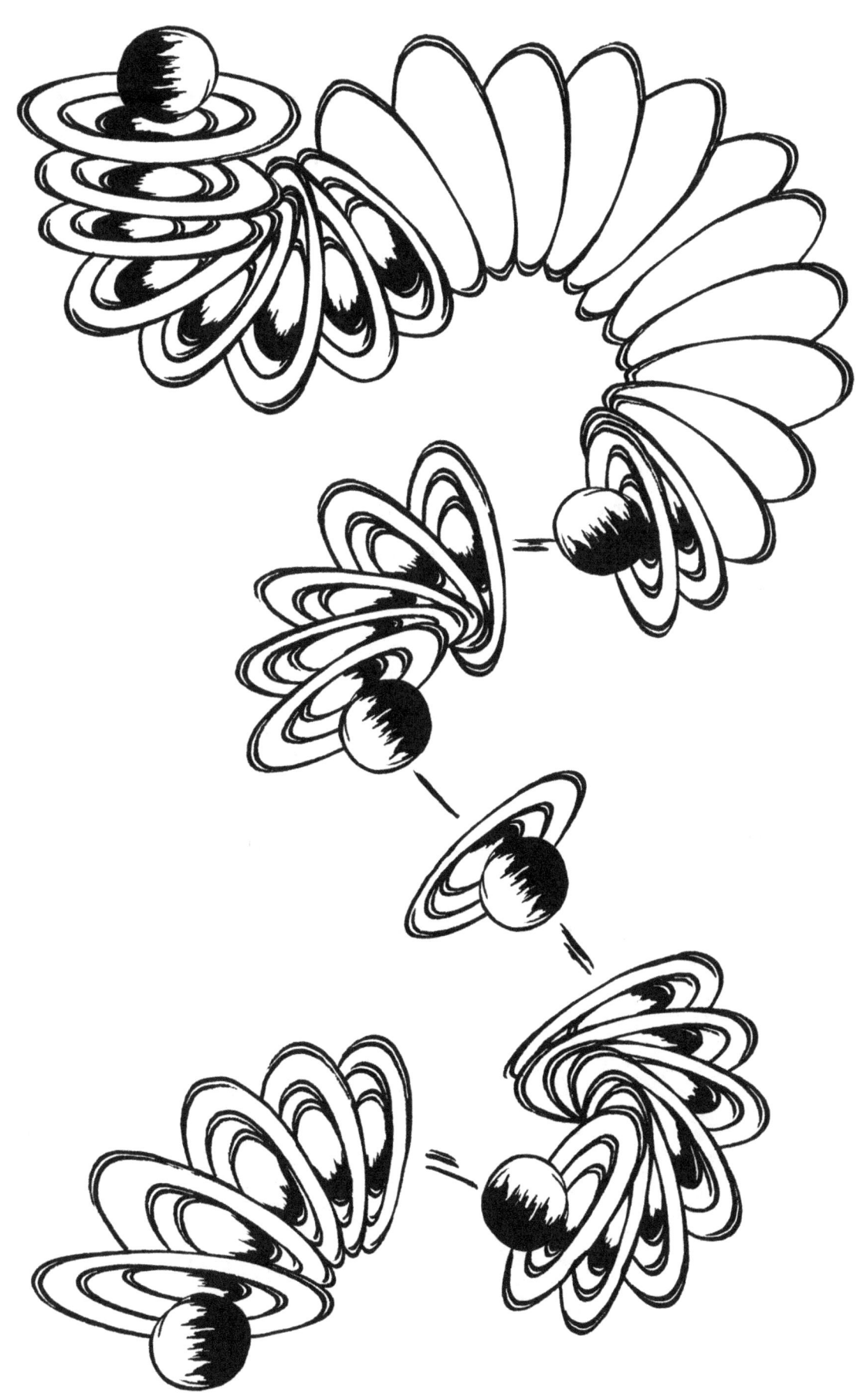

A doubtful friend is worse than a certain enemy. Let a man be one thing or the other, and we then know how to meet him.

Better be wise by the misfortunes of others than by your own.

In critical moments even the very powerful have need of the weakest.

It is thrifty to prepare today for the wants of tomorrow.

-- Aesop (620 BC - 560 BC)

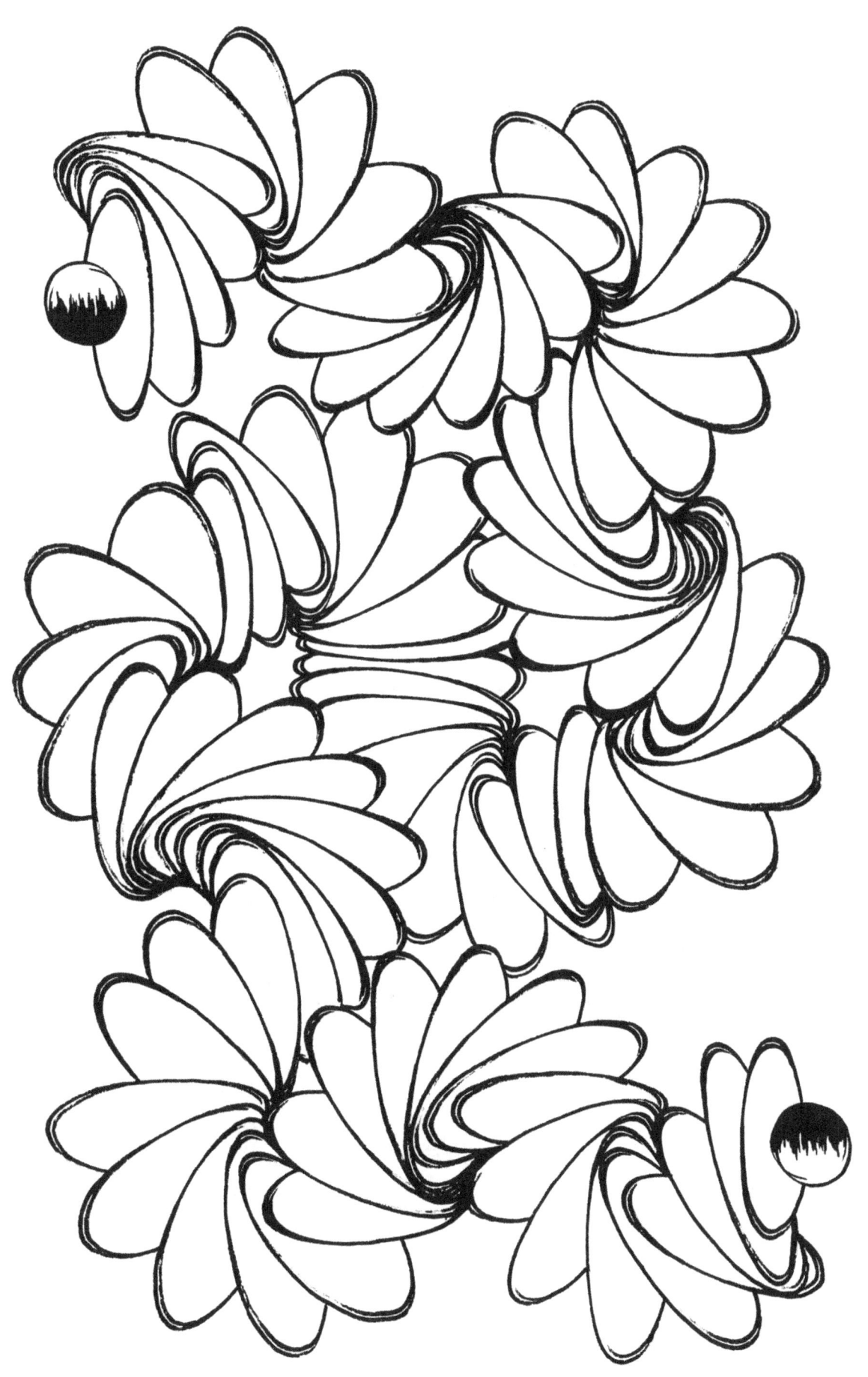

Events will take their course, it is no good of being angry at them; he is happiest who wisely turns them to the best account.

Wealth stays with us a little moment if at all: only our characters are steadfast, not our gold.

Short is the joy that guilty pleasure brings.

Do not consider painful what is good for you.

Waste not fresh tears over old grief.

Your very silence shows you agree.

A bad beginning makes a bad ending.

Talk sense to a fool and he calls you foolish.

-- Euripides (484 BC - 406 BC)

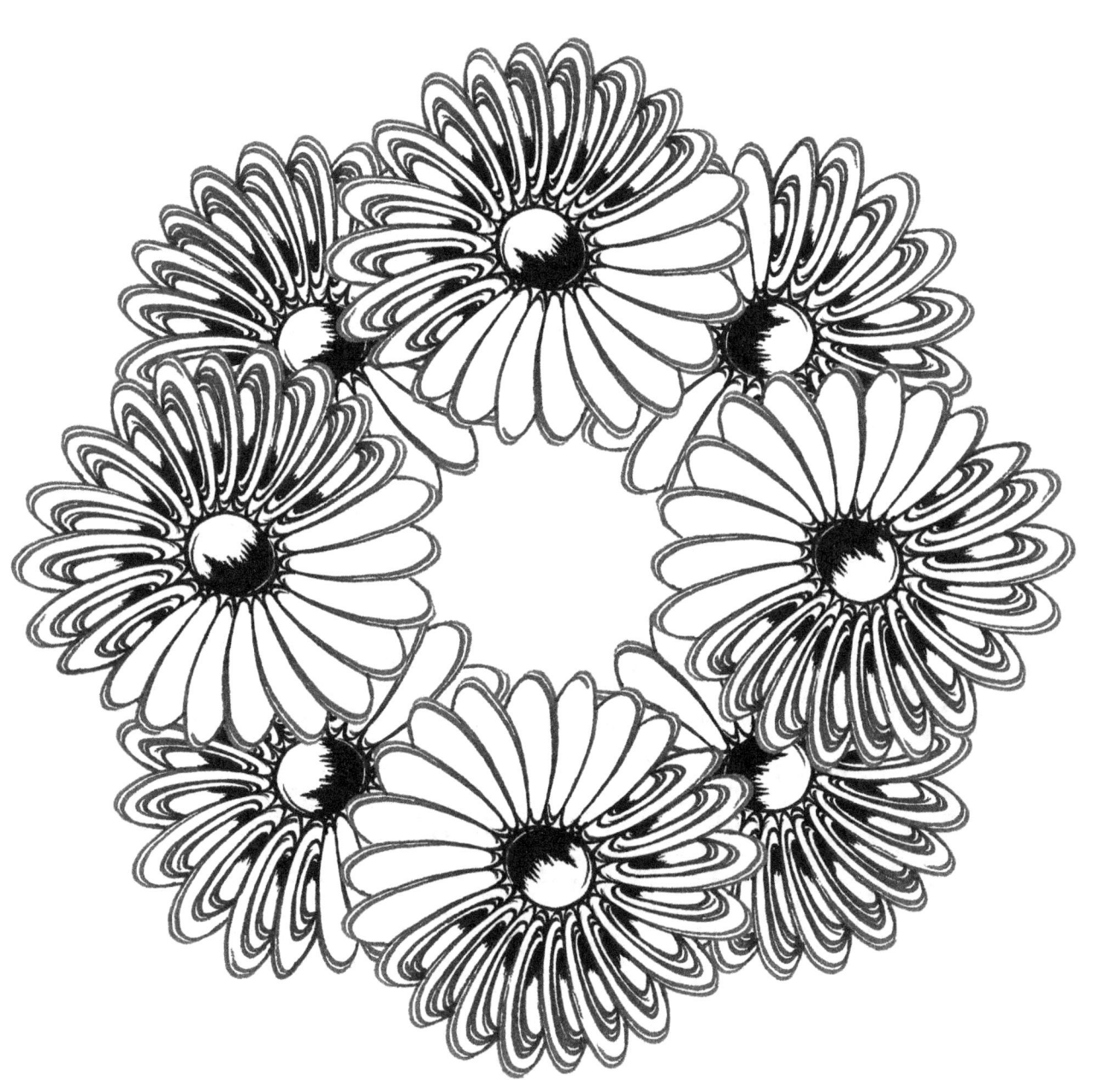

In a change of masters the poor change nothing except their master's name.

The humble suffer when the mighty disagree.

There is danger in both belief and unbelief.

Men in however high a station ought to fear the humble.

Aggression unchallenged is aggression unleashed.

It is destruction to the weak man to attempt to imitate the powerful.

-- Phaedrus (15 BC - 50 AD)

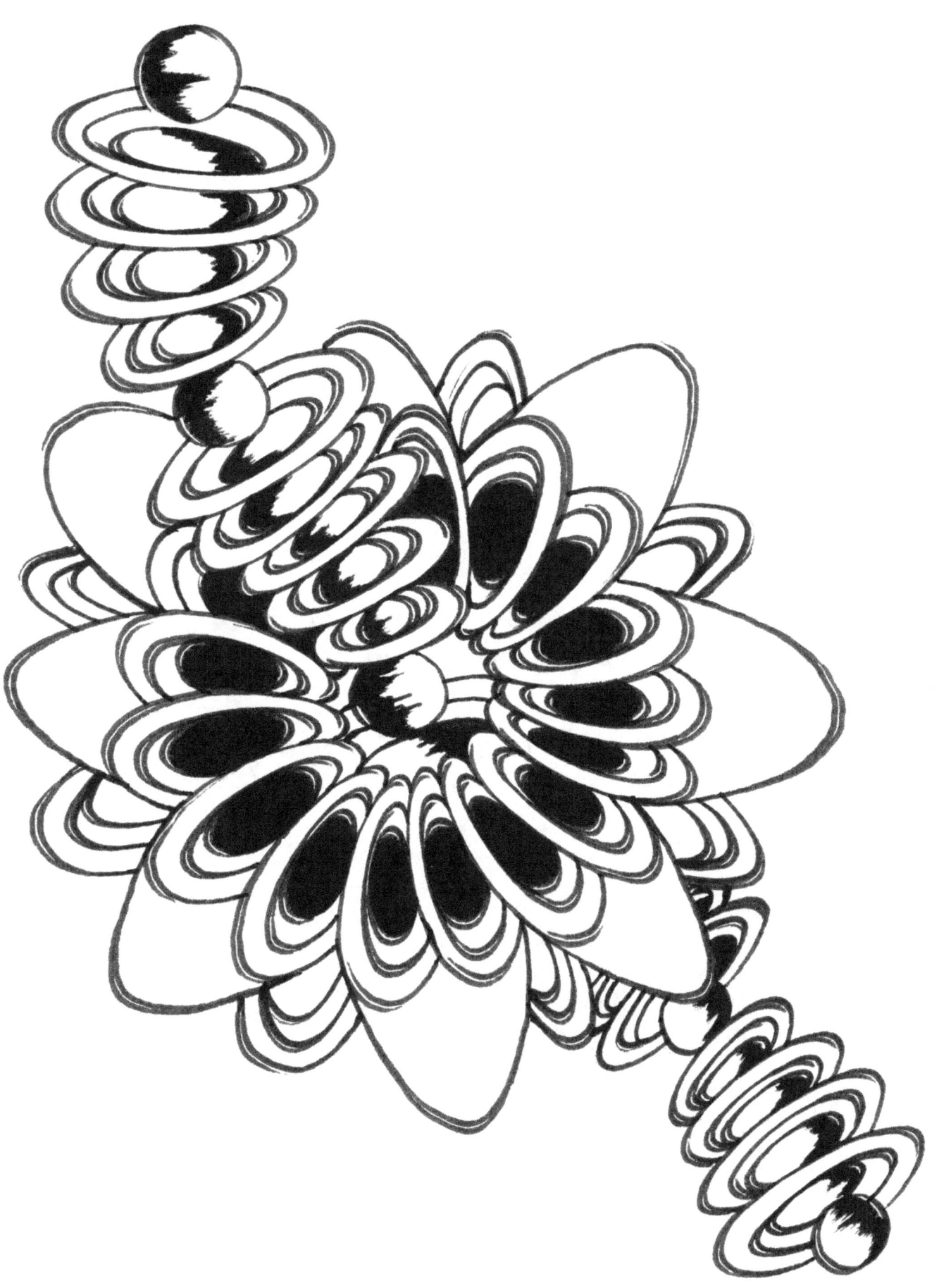

A man's character is his fate.

No man ever steps in the same river twice, for it's not the same river and he's not the same man.

-- Heraclitus (540 BC - 480 BC)

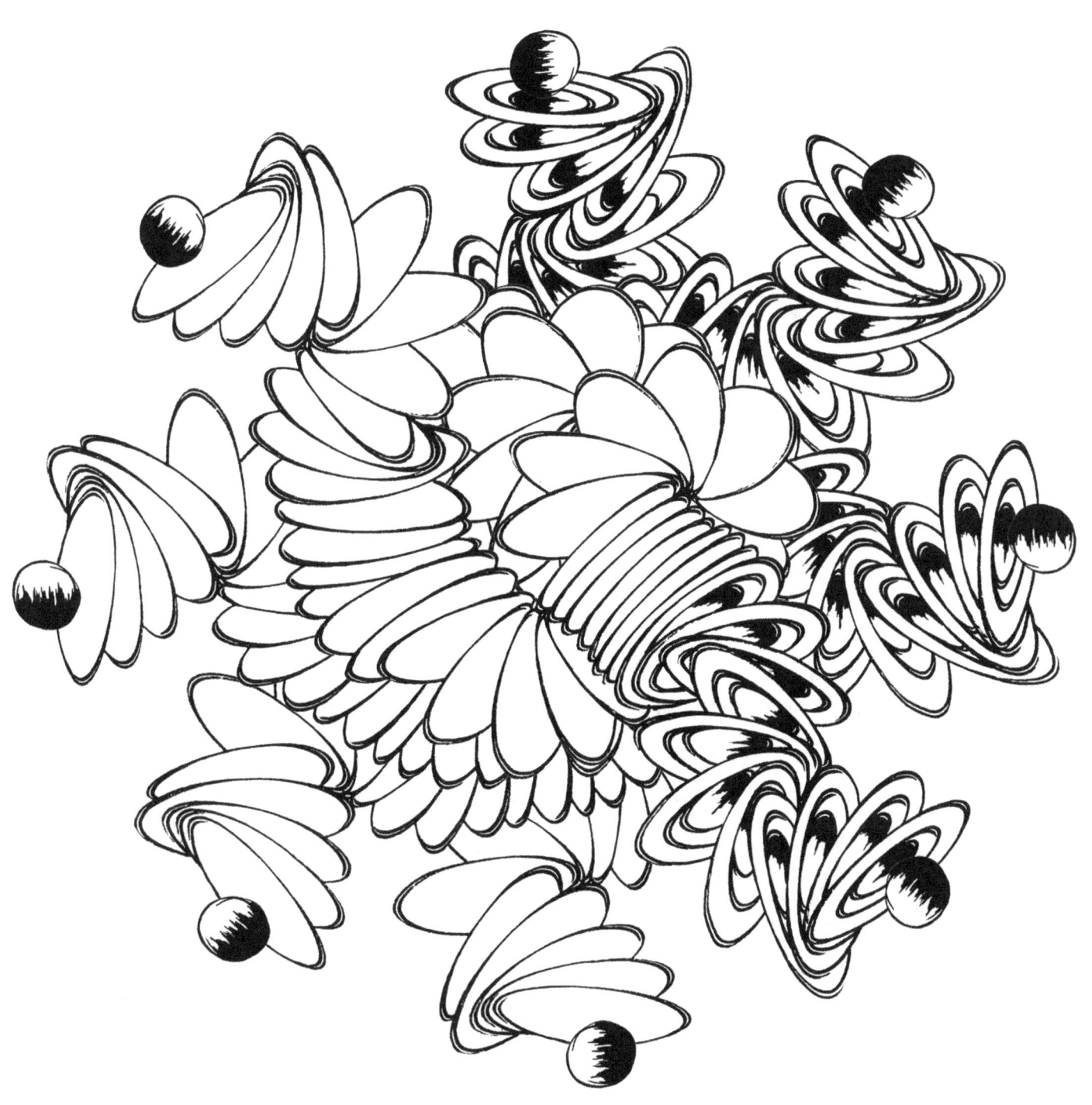

Nothing exists except atoms and empty space; everything else is opinion.

By desiring little, a poor man makes himself rich.

Do not trust all men, but trust men of worth; the former course is silly, the latter a mark of prudence.

Hope of ill gain is the beginning of loss.

If thou suffer injustice, console thyself; the true unhappiness is in doing it.

Now as of old the gods give men all good things, excepting only those that are baneful and injurious and useless. These, now as of old, are not gifts of the gods: men stumble into them themselves because of their own blindness and folly.

The wrongdoer is more unfortunate than the man wronged.

  -- Democritus 460 BC ~ 370 BC Greek

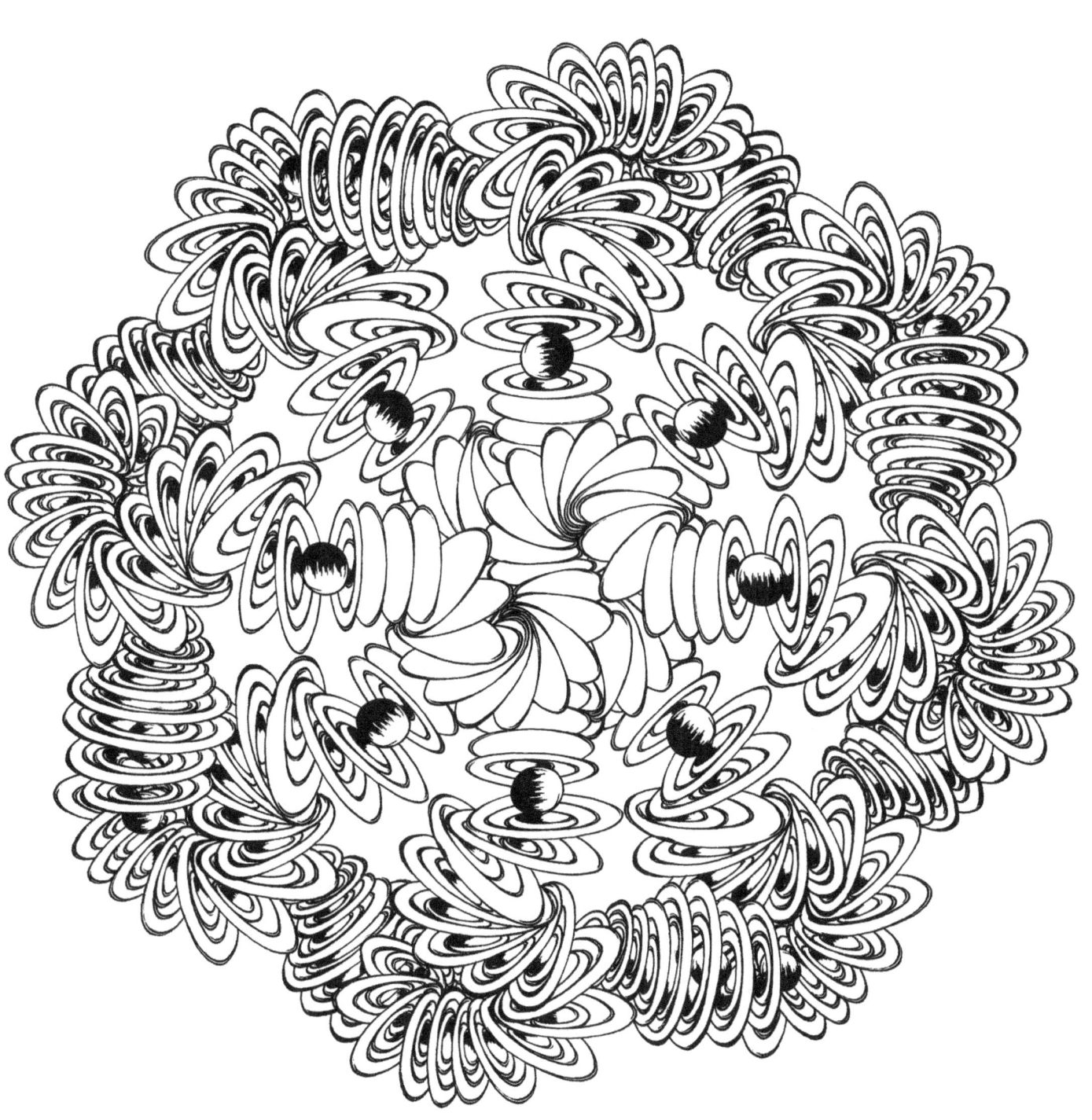

A woman's greatest glory is to be little talked about by men, whether for good or ill.

Wait for that wisest of all counselors, Time.

Fishes live in the sea, as men do on land: the great ones eat up the little ones.

For famous men have the whole earth as their memorial.

Trees, though they are cut and lopped, grow up again quickly, but if men are destroyed, it is not easy to get them again.

-- Pericles (490 BC - 429 BC)

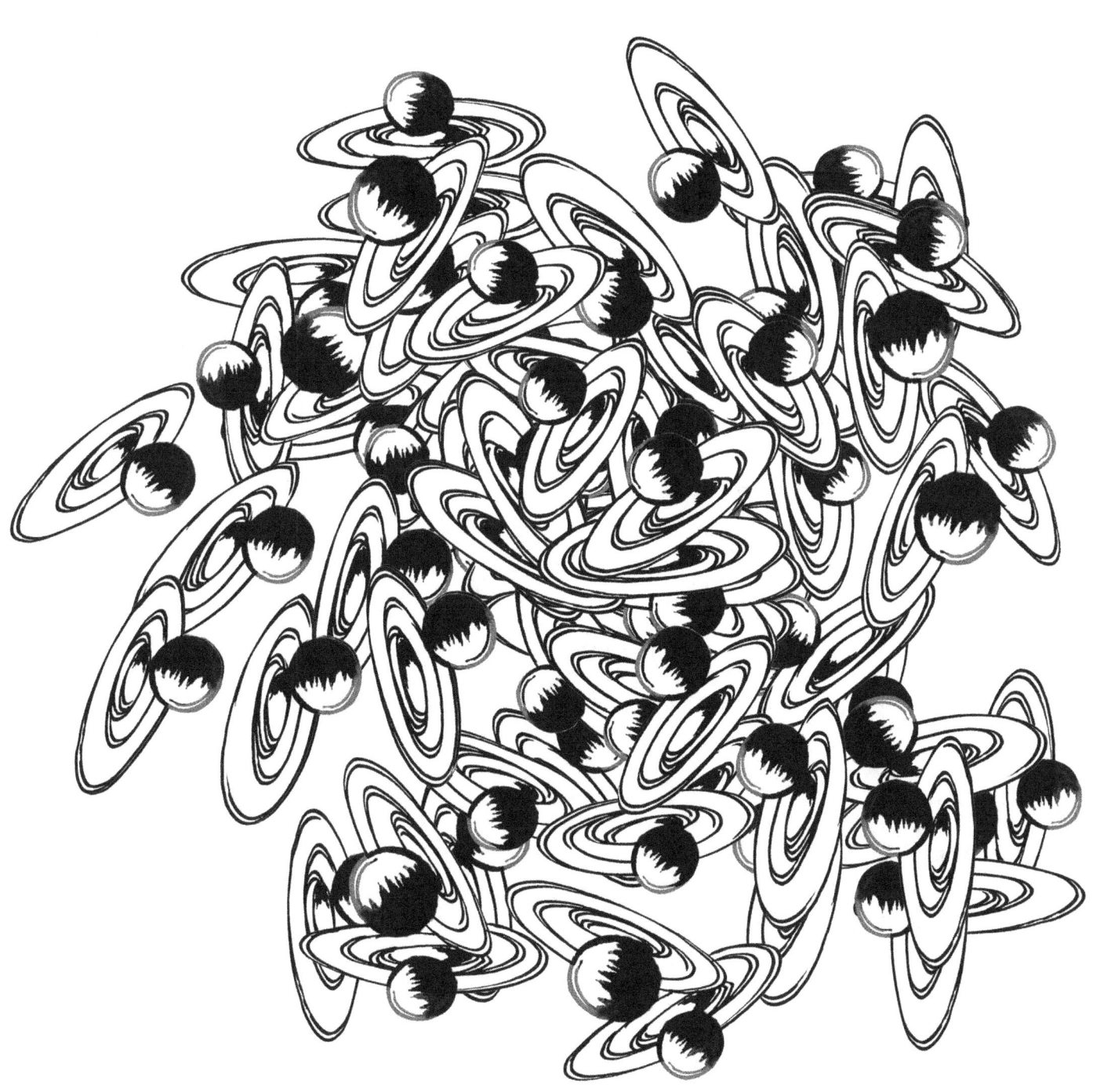

Anything is possible

   Sincerely,

Everything

   -- Argo Ink (1964 – present)

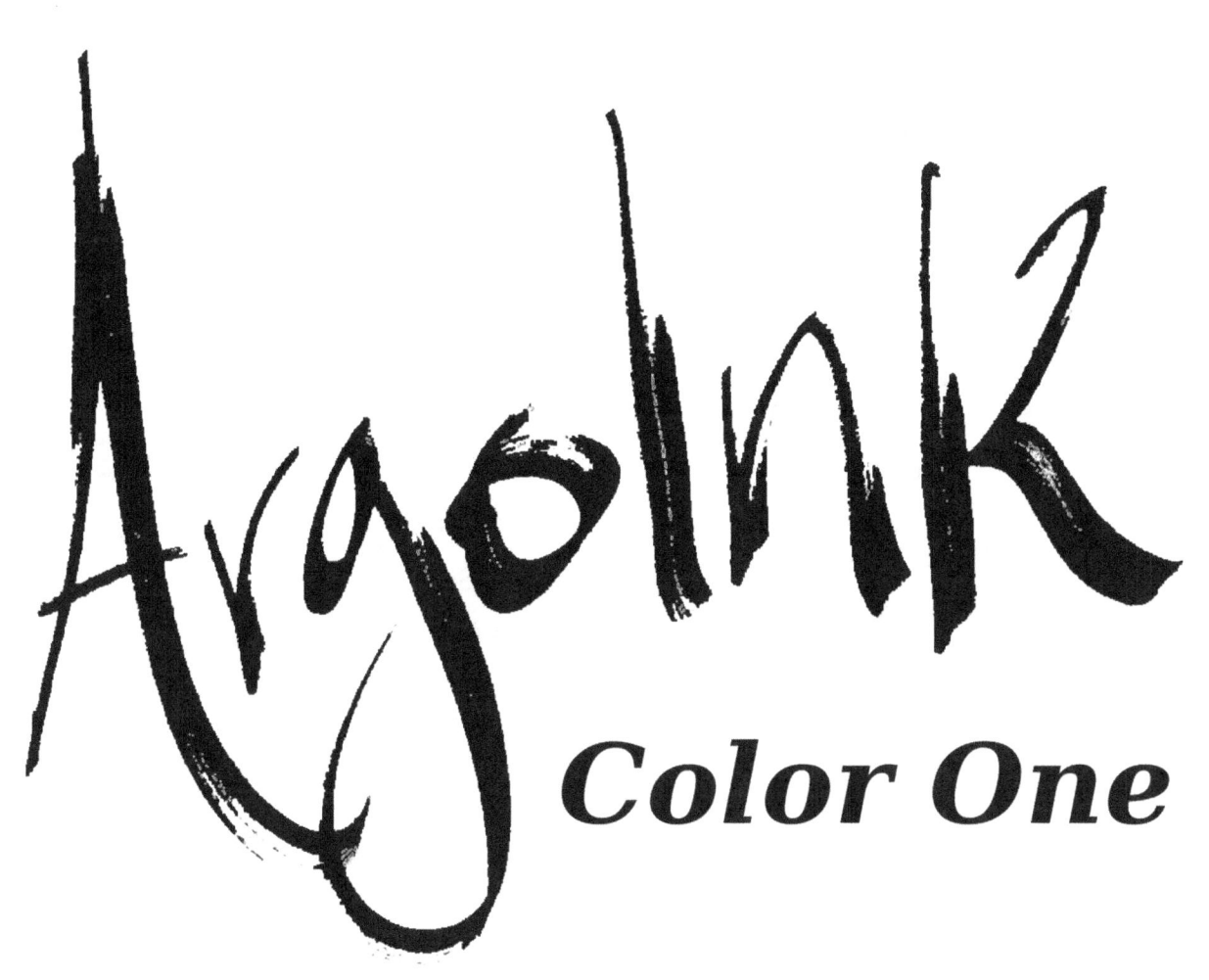

Color One

All ArgoInk products are available at 50% off their normal retail price when purchased for school and charitable fundraising events.

Please visit our web site for more details.

www.ArgoInk.com

www.ingramcontent.com/pod-product-compliance
Lightning Source LLC
Chambersburg PA
CBHW081419170526
45166CB00010B/3400

* 9 7 8 1 4 6 8 1 5 0 6 8 1 *